Original title:
The Jungle Within

Copyright © 2025 Creative Arts Management OÜ
All rights reserved.

Author: Julian Carmichael
ISBN HARDBACK: 978-1-80581-774-1
ISBN PAPERBACK: 978-1-80581-301-9
ISBN EBOOK: 978-1-80581-774-1

Whirlpools of Thought and Tree

In my mind, a monkey swings,
Chasing dreams with silly things.
Banana peels that slip and slide,
Giggles echo, can't hide inside.

A parrot squawks in vibrant hues,
Painting thoughts in wacky views.
While ants march in a line so neat,
With tiny boots, they shuffle their feet.

Vines twist tales, they can't be tamed,
Each loop a giggle, yet unnamed.
A treasure map of twists and quirks,
Where laughter bounces, never lurks.

So come along, let's play pretend,
In this land where sillies blend.
With whirlpools of thought, we'll dance and sway,
In our wild minds, we'll always stay.

Uncharted Echoes

In shadows deep, where tickles creep,
A squirrel jokes, while pandas leap.
The vines all swing, like dancers woo,
And every leaf holds gossip too.

A parrot squawks in vibrant hue,
'Hey you, don't step there, that's my loo!'
The crickets play a midnight tune,
While chaos reigns beneath the moon.

Secrets of the Canopy

Beneath the green, the secrets hide,
Where monkeys play, and sloths abide.
They share their tales of stolen snacks,
And gossip 'bout those cheeky hacks.

The toucan's beak is quite the sight,
It munches fruit late in the night.
While frogs in hats throw dance parades,
Their hops a riot in leafy shades.

Heartbeats of the Wild

The hummingbirds flash like laughter bright,
While jaguars nap, what a silly sight!
Chipmunks debate on who's got style,
And every twig points to a smile.

A turtle mutters, 'Life's too fast!'
As crabs on stilts flee from a cast.
The wild beats drum in playful jest,
As critters prank the clueless quest.

Whispers in the Thicket

In thickets lush, whispers abound,
Of foxes cracking jokes all around.
A snake, with flair, slinks past a tree,
And laughs at how weird life can be.

The beetles host a dinner dance,
With tiny tuxes, oh how they prance!
While ants, in sync, march to their song,
In this wild world, we all belong.

Tendrils of Hidden Truth

In the depths of the mind, thoughts twist and twine,
Like vines that entangle, so tricky and fine.
Silly secrets dangle, like fruit from a tree,
Waiting for someone to giggle with glee.

Monkeys swing wildly, no cares in their day,
While I trip on my thoughts, in a comical way.
Laughter erupts as I chase after clues,
But the truth seems to hide, in its own little snooze.

Echoing Footsteps in the Rainforest

In a forest so lush, where shadows confide,
I shuffle on quietly, as big bugs would glide.
Each footstep I take, makes a squishy, loud sound,
While the crickets all giggle, their laughter unbound.

A parrot squawks lessons, in a voice loud and clear,
But I can't seem to focus; I eavesdrop on fear.
The more I discover, the sillier it seems,
Like chasing my thoughts, in a world of wild dreams.

Flight of the Inner Eagle

An eagle within me, just wants to soar high,
But instead I'm stuck here, with a pie in the sky.
I flap my funny wings, create a ruckus and cheer,
While no one believes that I'm truly sincere.

With each soaring effort, I stumble and fall,
In laughter I gather my courage, I call.
The winds may be wild, but I'll play in the breeze,
Pretending to fly, with the greatest of ease.

A Canopy of Hidden Aspirations

Under leaves of ambition, I stretch and I bend,
Hoping my dreams like vines will extend.
I whisper to trees my most whimsical goals,
While they chuckle softly, with gnarled, leafy knolls.

The sun plays peek-a-boo, between branches so thick,
As I tumble through laughter, with great acrobatic trick.
For a canopy's shade holds a world full of fun,
Where wishes run wild, like a runaway bun.

Embrace of the Wild Unknown

In the forest of my mind, I roam,
Bumps and giggles lead me home.
Trees giggle as I trip and fall,
Silly creatures start to crawl.

A raccoon wears a fancy hat,
Sipping tea, on a welcome mat.
Monkeys swing with a cheeky grin,
Pointing, laughing, in a spin.

A lion's roar is just a sneeze,
Chasing shadows, swaying trees.
The parrot squawks a silly tune,
Dancing under the laughing moon.

In this madness, I find my peace,
Every giggle seems to increase.
Nature's playground brings delight,
In the wild, I laugh all night.

Patterns of Primal Essence

Patterns swirl like a dancing sprite,
Bellyaches from giggles in the night.
Lions prance in neon shoes,
While owls tell jokes I can't refuse.

A sloth tried yoga, fell on its back,
While penguins join in with a little quack.
Parrots gossip in the trees,
Spreading tales like a warm breeze.

Hippos munch on popcorn bliss,
While mosquitoes join in, swinging their fists.
A bear in shades plays the sax,
Swinging to tunes that never relax.

In the chaos, laughter brews,
Every moment, something new.
Nature's quirks are here to stay,
Making each wild moment play.

Breathe Among the Wildflowers

Wildflowers giggle, swaying bright,
Twirling bees in a dizzy flight.
A gopher's fashions are quite a sight,
Wearing socks that match the light.

Tickled by whispers of the breeze,
I sneak a peek at the dancing bees.
Daisies nod as I walk by,
In a silly world, I laugh and sigh.

Butterflies wear the latest trends,
While frogs hop in, making friends.
A beetle winks in a top hat,
Sipping nectar while sitting flat.

In this garden of joyful glee,
Nature's laughter calls to me.
Every petal tells a joke,
Among the flowers, laughter's smoke.

Songs of the Inner Savanna

In the savanna, a choir sings,
Of zebras talking and silly things.
A cheetah trips over its own tail,
While elephants dance, without fail.

Rhinos whistle a happy tune,
While gazelles leap beneath the moon.
Giraffes necking, oh what a sight,
Trying hard not to start a fight.

Warthogs giggle in muddy delights,
Chasing sunsets, reaching new heights.
Every jump brings a slapstick twist,
As nature's humor comes to assist.

With laughter echoing in the dusk,
Every moment, a joyful husk.
In this land of whimsical play,
Every creature knows how to sway.

An Inner Landscape of Leaves

In my mind, a tree does dance,
With rubber boots, it takes a chance.
Squirrels wear hats, they twirl with glee,
While butterflies sip on green tea.

The flowers sing in silly tune,
Bouncing like a cartoon raccoon.
They play hopscotch on carpet mounds,
As laughing frogs jump all around.

Within this space, the shadows grin,
A sloth steals cookies with a grin.
The grass tickles, adding to the fun,
As creatures chat beneath the sun.

Oh, what a sight, this playful maze,
Where every turn, a laugh, a craze!
In this leafy world of dreams and cheer,
The mind's wild corners feel so near.

Majesty of the Inner Beasts

Lions in bow ties strut the floor,
While penguins waltz and ask for more.
A zebra's stripes spell out a joke,
And all the mice wear silly cloak.

The parrot tells the latest news,
In a voice that tickles, not to snooze.
Giraffes stretch tall for the best view,
Sipping lemonade, they are a crew.

The tigers host a dance-off night,
With funky moves, they steal the sight.
Baboons juggle acorns with flair,
While elephants play tag without a care.

Such kingdom rules with laughter bright,
Where every critter brings delight.
Inside this realm that's vastly grand,
Truly, it's a beastly wonderland!

Riddles of the Ancient Grove

In ancient wood, a riddle plays,
A squirrel's worth its nuts, always.
The mushrooms whisper secrets low,
Who knew they could steal the show?

A wise old owl gives shrugging looks,
While porcupines write storybooks.
They share their tales of silly fights,
And giggles echo through the nights.

Each tree has eyes that ever peek,
At dancing shadows, playful sneak.
Laughter sprinkles, like rain from leaves,
In this enchanted place, one believes.

The riddle's edge is all in jest,
As turtles host a goofy fest.
Through winding paths, the laughter flows,
The ancient grove's not short on prose.

Secrets Beneath the Twisting Vines

Beneath the vines, where whispers creep,
A rabbit dreams and takes a leap.
With sunglasses on, he makes a scene,
And ice cream drips—what a routine!

The tangled roots hold secrets rare,
As snails trade jokes without a care.
Grasshoppers throw confetti high,
In colors bright against the sky.

A wise old snake times every pun,
With giggles floating, all in fun.
The hedgehogs roll in vegetable balls,
While laughter echoes, joy enthralls.

So wander down this wiggly path,
Where each twist turns to hearty laugh.
Among the vines, a playful sway,
Secrets tumble, brightening the day.

Shadows of the Leaf

In the depths of green, I trip and fall,
A squirrel laughs, and I hear it call.
I'm lost in the weeds, a tangled mess,
The flowers chuckle, I must confess.

Lizards wiggle like they own the place,
While I just hope to find my face.
Brambles tease, they know how to play,
This leafy world just won't be tamed today.

Soul of the Untamed

The raccoons gather for a late-night feast,
They steal my snacks, nature's little beast.
I dance with shadows, hop like a hare,
Who needs a partner? I've got fresh air!

Overgrown plants, they wiggle and sway,
I'm a wild explorer, but I lose my way.
The owls start hooting, a nightly cheer,
While I just giggle, with no hint of fear.

Beneath the Verdant Veil

Beneath the canopy, I spot a clown,
A frog in a bowtie, oh, what a frown!
With every leap, he jumps my way,
Singing silly songs, brightening my day.

Butterflies flutter, in colors so bright,
They laugh at my hair, all wild in the night.
Tangled grass tickles my unsuspecting feet,
They join the fun, it's quite the treat!

Footprints in the Wilderness

I leave shiny prints in mud and goo,
The slugs wave back with their slimy cue.
I take a detour through bushes and brambles,
Finding lost treasures, or so my heart scrambles.

Creatures peek out, with eyes full of glee,
"Look at that human, so lost in the spree!"
They chuckle together at my funny plight,
In this wild playground, everything feels right.

Vines of Inner Turmoil

In my head, a jungle swings,
Vines of thoughts with many flings.
A monkey jokes, I laugh along,
But oh! This chatter feels so wrong.

Lions lounge, they take a snack,
While I ponder what I lack.
The toucan squawks, what a delight,
Yet I just can't seem to write.

A parrot mocks my every scheme,
Trapped in this chaotic dream.
Bushes rustle with my doubts,
Made of whispers, fears, and shouts.

Oh, tangled vines of silly strife,
Turn my thoughts to comic life.
In this wild, I find my game,
Laughing as I stake my claim.

Rhythm of the Wild Spirit

A beat is drumming, birds all swoop,
To the rhythm of the wild troop.
Squirrels dance and swing about,
What's it all really about?

Bouncing frogs share silly songs,
While crickets chirp with scratchy gongs.
Inside my chest, the beat goes boom,
Like a party in my room!

Giraffes groove with legs so long,
While cockatoos sing loud and strong.
The trees sway to this funny tune,
In my heart, there's a cartoon!

So let's shake it, twirl, and spin,
Dance beneath the leafy din.
Every creature finds delight,
In the rhythm, all feels right!

Dance of the Hidden Beasts

In the shadows, creatures peek,
A lively dance, it's quite unique.
A hedgehog spins, a crab does prance,
With every move, they take a chance.

Zebras trot with stripes so bold,
In moonlit glades, their stories told.
A sloth does the slow-motion glide,
Cracking jokes while they reside.

Tigers twirl in sheer surprise,
Just as friendly as they're wise.
While owls chuckle through the night,
Unmasking tricks without a fright.

Oh, hidden beasts of every kind,
In their dance, pure joy we find.
Under starlit skies, they prance,
As laughter leads this bright romance.

Lurking in the Thicket

With stealth, I creep through leafy space,
Where giggles echo, without a trace.
The raccoons plot their cheeky game,
While I join in, it's all the same.

Behind the ferns, a fox peeks out,
With a mischievous, playful shout.
He swoops and dives, it's such a sight,
In this thicket, all feels right.

Caterpillars crawl in funky lines,
As butterflies wear flashy signs.
A grasshopper jumps, oh what a leap,
Tickling roots and causing a heap!

In this realm where secrets dwell,
Funny moments cast their spell.
Lurking here brings pure delight,
In thickets where mischief ignites.

Flickers of Light Among Shadows

In the thicket, things go bump,
Squirrels dance and trees go thump.
The sun peeks through a leafy crown,
While I trip on roots—oh, what a clown!

Laughter echoes in the green,
As vines sway like a silly scene.
A parrot squawks with all its might,
While I search for snacks, what a plight!

Unruly curls of ivy tease,
While frogs croak out their symphonies.
A deer prances in polka dots,
Finding my snacks—now that's just hot!

So here I skip and juggle trees,
Talking to bugs, just me and bees.
Embracing chaos as it flies,
With giggles bursting from wild highs!

A Tapestry of Unseen Creatures

Beneath the leaf, a party's brewing,
With beetles dancing, all pursuing.
A snail in shades of full couture,
Wears glimmering shells that just endure.

The bees are gossiping like mad,
While ants are organizing—what a fad!
A rabbit in a tiny hat,
Rides on a turtle, fancy that!

Invisible friends all around,
Whispering secrets without a sound.
The butterflies plot a fashion show,
While I try to blend in with the flow!

With every rustle, a giggle pops,
As nature plays its sneaky chops.
In this lively and funny spree,
I fit right in, just wild and free!

Bound by the Roots of Existence

Roots entangled like a game of Twister,
While fronds tickle, a leafy sister.
Tree trunks wearing mossy hats,
Chatting with crows and playful bats.

A wise old oak shares ancient tales,
Of pranks pulled by clever snails.
Grasshoppers leap as if in flight,
Sprinkling laughter through day and night.

The shadows dance, a quirky crew,
Whispering jokes just for a few.
My feet stumble on the winding paths,
Only to land in muddy baths!

Together we laugh beneath the sun,
In this wild mess, we're all just fun.
Nature's comedy, stitched with cheer,
Reminds us that joy is always near!

Harmony in the Chaotic Wild

In the heart of chaos, a tune takes shape,
With monkeys swinging in silly drape.
The parrots squawk in vibrant hues,
While I mimic, just a wild ruse.

A lion yawns, it's nap time still,
Dreaming of snacks and juicy thrills.
The zebras strut in monochrome,
Making a fashion statement, far from home.

A hippo joins the dance parade,
Creating splashes with a grand charade.
As laughter echoes through tall grass,
Nature's punchlines fly and amass.

With critters jiving and all entwined,
There's a magic that lightens the mind.
In this ruckus, I fit just right,
Embracing the fun of every night!

Whispers of the Untamed Wind

In shadows where the humor sings,
A monkey jester pulls at strings.
With giggles wrapped in vibrant green,
He steals the show, a comic scene.

The parrot shouts with vibrant tone,
Telling jokes to the trees alone.
Laughter bounces in the air,
While squirrels dance without a care.

The sneaky fox, with clever style,
Tells puns that make the tigers smile.
In the thicket, gales conspire,
To tickle all with funny fire.

As twilight drapes the leafy dome,
The critters gather, far from home.
With punchlines woven in the leaves,
They share their tales with all who cleave.

Roots of an Unseen World

Beneath the earth where shadows dwell,
A dancing root begins to swell.
With wiggly moves, it shakes the ground,
And laughs as all the bugs surround.

The earthworm wears a fancy hat,
While telling tales of wild chitchat.
A beetle on a tiny stage,
Performs a play with comical rage.

The roots entwine in playful cheer,
As whispers of their antics steer.
Gossip spreads like leafy vines,
About the pranks of ancient times.

In layers deep, where secrets hide,
The laughter rolls, it can't reside.
From soil thick, to skies so bright,
The fun takes root in pure delight.

Explorations of the Heart's Wilderness

In the wilds of a heart so free,
A fox dons boots, oh what a spree!
With compasses made of silly string,
He ventures out to see what's king.

A squirrel reads a treasure map,
While giggling loud, a joyful clap.
With acorns as their golden loot,
They celebrate with silly hoot.

Around each bend, a mystery waits,
With critters dressed in funny States.
They play charades, a feathery crew,
Each motion bright, and grand debut.

In playful quests of heart and mind,
They seek the joy that's hard to find.
With every laugh, they bloom anew,
In their wild land, adventures brew.

The Wild Within the Heart

In chambers where the laughter grows,
A lion prances in footy clothes.
With every roar a tickle fight,
His mane as wild as day turns night.

Tigers juggle with fierce delight,
While zebras dance in black and white.
Each step a burst of quirky grace,
They twirl and spin, a vibrant race.

With every thump of joyful heart,
A symphony of quirky art.
In this domain of giggling cheer,
The wildest dreams all reappear.

The forest friends, they lend a hand,
To keep the fun, both bright and grand.
In every beat, the rhythm flows,
In the wild heart where laughter glows.

Layers of Inner Wilderness

Beneath my skin, a critter's ball,
Where inner monkeys often call.
They swing and jump, they act absurd,
In my mind's park, they flap and herd.

A squirrel sneaks for midnight snacks,
While I chase dreams, he hides in cracks.
I laugh at roars that shake my brain,
One day I'll tame this wild domain.

Each thought a vine, tangling tight,
I dance between the wrong and right.
With bee-sized thoughts that buzz and hum,
Inside this maze, I'm all but dumb.

So here I sit, my psyche's stew,
A cocktail mix of brave and blue.
Yet when I grin and dive right in,
I find the wild is where I win.

Heartstrings Amongst the Thorns

My heart strings twang like rubber bands,
Amidst the thorns with pointy hands.
Each prick a note, I play along,
In this rough patch, I sing my song.

The roses blush, they whisper low,
"Hey, watch your step, the hedges grow!"
I dodge and weave like dancers do,
In this wild maze, I'm lost but true.

A cactus winks, it's not so tough,
Words of wisdom—man, it's rough!
With every scrape and every fall,
I find the humor in it all.

So let me laugh, with joy I'll bounce,
Amongst the pricks, my heart just flounces.
Because with each thorn, my spirit roars,
In this wild play, my humor soars.

Navigating Through the Wilds of Self

In the forest of my thoughts, I stroll,
With signs that say, 'Mind your soul!'
A grumpy deer blocks my way,
I offer cookies, and make him sway.

Here's a river of self-doubt's flow,
I skip a stone, giving it a go.
It splashes wide, I laugh and grin,
This journey's wild, but I can swim.

An owl hoots wise from a tree,
"Don't take it all too seriously!"
I wave at shadows, jest and spin,
For in this wild, I always win.

With each step, I gain a clue,
A compass made of laughs—who knew?
Through every twist and every bend,
I find the fun has no end.

Disturbances in the Thicket

Within the thicket, chaos reigns,
As branches dance like wild canes.
A raccoon shouts, "What's going on?"
I trip and tumble, yet I yawn.

The bushes rustle, secrets tease,
A sneaky fox says, "Hey, let's squeeze!"
I squeeze right back, we share a laugh,
In this wild game, I've found my path.

A rooster crows, it's far from dawn,
But here I am, a merry pawn.
With hiccups loud and antics bright,
The forest plays, a silly sight.

So join this romp, let's raise some noise,
In this thick mess, we'll find our joys.
For every snare, there's humor sown,
Together wild, we've truly grown.

Heartbeats Beneath the Canopy

In the leafy depths, the critters play,
Cats in costumes, prancing away.
A squirrel juggles acorns with flair,
While a sloth complains, 'Life's just not fair.'

Beneath great vines, a party in sight,
Bugs wear tuxedos, ready for the night.
Frogs pull pranks, as they leap and croak,
Even the crickets have learned to smoke.

A parrot squawks jokes, oh what a crowd!
While beetles are dancing, feeling quite proud.
With laughter and glee, the hours go by,
Who knew the wild could tickle the sky?

But just as the fun reaches its peak,
A catnip-induced dream makes them all squeak.
And when morning rings, the laughter wears thin,
Yet, behind every leaf, they'll do it again!

Secrets of the Hidden Wild

In shadows deep, the secrets remain,
A chameleon painted like a candy cane.
A raccoon whispers tales of a heist,
While owls roll their eyes, unimpressed, not nice.

The ants scheme grand plans for their picnics,
As spiders weave webs in the shape of gimmicks.
A fox tells the tale of a brave little mouse,
Who captured the cheese and hid in her house.

The wind carries giggles through tangled vines,
While monkeys swing high on invisible lines.
In this hidden realm, all jest and jest,
With laughter so bright, who needs any rest?

But as dusk descends, the giggles may wane,
Yet tomorrow's secrets will rise once again.
For in this wild, crazy and free,
The humor keeps blooming like leaves on a tree.

Fragments of Forgotten Wilderness

In a realm of green, where shadows collide,
A tortoise grins wide, says, "I take it in stride."
While the birds share gossip through fluttering wings,
About the odd habits of pesky old things.

Frogs on their lily pads, making loud bets,
Playing leapfrog while forgetting regrets.
A raccoon wearing shades steals berries from trees,
While a bear rolls by, summoning a breeze.

Laughter erupts like a bubbling brook,
As butterflies gossip in each little nook.
As sunbeams paint spots on the leafy green floor,
The critters keep chuckling, forever wanting more.

But twilight will whisper, "It's time to recline,"
Yet they'll meet again when the stars start to shine.
In fragments of wild, hidden from sight,
The laughter will linger till morning's first light.

Echoes of the Untamed Heart

In the thick of the night, where heroes are spun,
A llama serenades under the sun.
With a wink and a grin, it's a sight to behold,
As it regales tall tales that aren't ever told.

The hippos are chuckling, they toss and they roll,
While the parakeets gossip, losing control.
A party of iguanas sway with the beat,
While the tortoises shuffle, feeling quite fleet.

The echoes of laughter bounce off the trees,
As the night creatures dance on the energy breeze.
Under twinkling stars, they twist and they twirl,
In a carnival rhythm, the wilds all unfurl.

When dawn begins creeping, they'll rest their proud hearts,
But the joy of this night will never depart.
For the echoes will linger, a melody sweet,
In the heart of the wild, they're never discreet!

Essence of the Wildflower Path

In a garden where giggles sprout,
Bees wear shoes, buzzing about.
A frog croaks jokes on a lily pad,
While daisies laugh, how silly is that!

Butterflies dance with a cha-cha flair,
A hidden rabbit braids its hair.
Squirrels tell tales of nutty quests,
In this bloom of laughter, nature rests.

The wind cracks up as it weaves through trees,
Whispering secrets to the playful breeze.
Petals pirouette in the sun's warm glow,
Nature's comedy show in full flow!

So skip down this path, come join the cheer,
Where the wildflowers tickle, and all is dear.
With each twist and turn, a smile you'll find,
A giggle-fueled stroll in the wildflower mind.

Nature's Unquiet Mind

The brook is gabbing, oh what a chatter,
It spills its secrets, not a care in splatter.
Trees gossip softly with rustling leaves,
While ants debate, plotting their thievery heaves.

The owl jokes at midnight, wise and sleek,
While crickets share puns, so loud and meek.
A bear in pajamas sips herbal tea,
Musing on life and his foot-stuffed bee.

Monkeys swing by with a raucous cheer,
Flipping through branches, no cause for fear.
Nature's a stage, with acts so absurd,
In a world where even rocks have heard.

So let's toast the chaos, our wild friend's glee,
Here laughter is nectar, as sweet as can be.
When nature giggles, hearts unwind, oh so true,
In this unquiet mind, there's fun just for you!

Whispers of Untamed Souls

The fox tells tales of her nightly romps,
While turtles tickle with their slowest stomps.
A parrot cracks jokes, full of color and sass,
Laughing at passersby in the tall grass.

In moonlight's shimmer, shadows prance,
While beetles do the cha-cha as if by chance.
Every critter joins in, a lively spree,
Nature's own carnival, wild and free!

The flowers snicker at the wandering bee,
Who buzzes around without a decree.
Grasshoppers dance, their legs in a twist,
A kooky fiesta, you wouldn't want to miss!

So embrace the whispers, the chuckles so bright,
Untamed spirits frolic in the soft twilight.
In this whimsical realm where laughter's a goal,
Be lost in the joy of these untamed souls!

Shadows in the Underbrush

Beneath the leaves, where shadows play,
The raccoon's humor keeps night at bay.
With a wink and a grin, he dumpster dives,
Bringing laughter to all the critter lives.

A hedgehog rolls by, bursting with pride,
Telling stories of the ones he's spied.
The crickets chuckle with their tiny tune,
As the moon beams down, big as a balloon.

The nocturnal ballet, a comedy seen,
As fireflies glow, their dance quite keen.
In the underbrush, a light-hearted fuss,
Every critter conspires without a fuss.

So tiptoe softly, enjoy the sights,
For mischief brews in the starry nights.
Among shadows and giggles, joyfully swish,
Like the cheer in the heart of a woodland wish!

Embracing the Ferocity

In the heart of my chest, a beast does dance,
With wild little moves, it takes every chance.
It snoozes with snorts, then jumps with a roar,
Who knew my heart could be such a bore?

Snack time is chaos, it's a glycogen spree,
A banana's an enemy, just wait and see.
My stomach growls loud, the trees shake in fright,
As I munch through the jungle, an absurd appetite!

It's a party of ants with confetti at noon,
And the frogs serenade me with a silly tune.
I swat at the flies, they just laugh and tease,
In this feral affair, I'm the clown of the trees!

Swinging like monkeys, feeling so spry,
Who needs a gym when you can leap, oh my!
With leafy confetti and a vine for a tie,
I'm embracing the ferocity—let out a cry!

Dreams Behind the Vines

Among tangled dreams, where the wild things play,
My fluffy thoughts dance, and they twirl all day.
Coconut clouds float above my head,
While the sloths cheer me on from their leafy bed.

Sometimes I wonder, while scratching my chin,
If a parrot could sing, would it know how to grin?
But giggles erupt from the bush, oh so loud,
As a raccoon in sunglasses joins the crowd.

Beneath leafy covers, secrets are shared,
An owl in a bow tie candidly stared.
We talk of our dreams over leafy cuisine,
With laughter so hearty, it's fit for a queen!

The sun dips low, but the fun's just begun,
As I dance with the shadows, we'll bask in the sun.
In this vine-laden land, joy grows on each line,
Revelation of mischief—our dreams intertwine.

Tapestry of the Untamed

In the canvas of chaos, mischief takes flight,
With colors of giggles painted so bright.
A monkey's swing echoing pure bliss,
While the turtles contemplate—'Is this worth the risk?'

Got a caper planned with the squirrels so spry,
Building acorn towers to touch the sky.
And just when they think they've outsmarted me,
I trip on a vine—oh, sweet irony!

With laughter like bubbles that float through the air,
The deer chuckle softly, adornment of flair.
A raucous parade through the thicket spins round,
Each step turns a stumble, and joy knows no bound!

Cheeky critters merge in a jubilant swirl,
Twirling and swirling—a wacky squirrel whirl!
In this tapestry vibrant, both wild and free,
Even chaos finds rhythm—come dance with me!

Pulse of the Forest

The rhythm of leaves beats a syncopate tune,
With a critter-sized band playing under the moon.
The owls are the maestros, in silver crows' wings,
While fireflies flash like they're plucking at strings.

The beat drops low as a sloth joins the crew,
Shuffling his way, like, 'What else is new?'
A raccoon on maracas shakes all through the trees,
And the woeful old tree sings the low harmony.

With each thud of my foot, the ground starts to quake,
While the caiman plays bass—what a curious wake!
Cacophony echoing from branches alight,
In the forest's embrace, it's a whimsical night!

So come join the pulse, let's groove and misplay,
With laughter as our guide, we'll dance 'til the day.
From the bark's gentle hum to the leaves' hearty laugh,
In this wondrous wild rhythm, we've found our true path!

Stories from the Forgotten Grove

In a grove where whispers play,
Frogs wear shoes and dance all day.
Squirrels throw acorns like confetti,
While turtles strut with eyes all jetty.

A raccoon juggles with a can,
Beneath a tree that's vastly grand.
Laughter echoes, joy takes flight,
As day turns slowly into night.

A shadow swings from grapevine ropes,
While hedgehogs share their funny hopes.
"Why don't we put on a parade?
With carrots marching, unafraid!"

So in the grove, they sing and cheer,
With silly dreams and tons of gear.
Each tale told, a giggle spreads,
As nature spins her yarns in threads.

Chasing Shadows in the Foliage

In the trees, a shadow stirs,
Jumping high, an owl purrs.
Bunnies laugh as they hop about,
"Catch that whimsy, give a shout!"

Squirrels plotting in the boughs,
Scheme to take the picnic vows.
With peanut butter, bread, and jam,
The forest fills with squeaky wham!

A chipmunk dresses as a knight,
Polishing his acorn bright.
"Come forth, creatures, hear my quest,
To find our snacks—let's do our best!"

So as the sun dips low and slow,
The foliage sways with chortling glow.
Each shadow, each giggle takes flight,
In this woodland, pure delight.

The Serpent's Silent Glance

A serpent lounges on a rock,
With a sly smile and ticklish shock.
"Why don't we start a fashion spree?
With leaves and flowers, just for me!"

His buddies—frogs, lizards, too,
Gather round for a leafy brew.
Mixed drinks of dew and berry pie,
With fashion shows that make you sigh.

The serpent poses, strikes a pose,
In snaky flair, his scales will glow.
"Who knew slithering could be chic?
With style so bold—it's truly unique!"

A giggle echoes through the trees,
The forest sways in playful tease.
With each glance, a chuckle rings,
As nature laughs at all these things.

Cries of the Solitary Bird

In the branches, a lone bird sings,
His tunes are funny, flapping wings.
"Hey folks, did you hear my joke?
About the tree? It's quite the oak!"

Squirrels giggle, owls hoot loud,
As whispers creep beneath the cloud.
But he's not shy, with flair he quips,
"Why don't all trees wear fancy clips?"

In a chirpy voice, he spins a tale,
Of acorn pirates who set sail.
"Waving flags made of green leaves,
Raiding nests, oh what mischief!"

The laughter rises with the breeze,
As every critter bends their knees.
In his antics, joy unfurled,
The solitary bird charms the world.

Amongst the Leaves of Reflection

In the forest of my mind, I roam,
Chasing squirrels that call me home.
Reflections dance on branches bold,
While monkeys chatter secrets untold.

Beneath the shade where laughter grows,
I trip on roots, and it often shows.
A bear nearby hums a tune,
As I sip my thoughts like a cartoon.

Sunlight tickles the leaves above,
While I ponder life, a laugh, a shove.
Lions lounge with a lazy yawn,
Their roars a giggle at dawn's first fawn.

A parrot squawks my every blunder,
Reminding me not to take life under.
With bouncing steps, I skip and leap,
In this wild place, my soul takes a peep.

The Wild Soliloquy

In the thicket where whispers thrive,
I debate my snacks, who can survive?
Grapes or cookies? Oh, what a plight!
The cheeky raccoon snickers with delight.

A bear shows off his dance moves next,
I try to join; it's quite perplexed.
As vines entangle my flailing feet,
Even the sloths can't help but greet.

Chirping crickets form a band,
While I juggle thoughts, very unplanned.
My jokes go wild, like a monkey's screech,
Nature roars back, it's quite the reach!

In this circus of flora and fun,
Every wild creature knows how to run.
So I'll laugh and tumble till day is done,
In this soliloquy, I've truly won.

Currents of Uncharted Feelings

Through vines of thought, I mostly drift,
Stumbling over a frond, how gift!
My heart is a river, absurd and wild,
Waiting for wisdom, just like a child.

I found a snail with dreams quite grand,
He wants to travel to a distant land.
A frog in a top hat leaps with flair,
Singing of journeys, unaware how rare.

Bouncing breezes laugh at my quest,
With each misstep, I feel truly blessed.
The turtles play chess with thoughts so deep,
While I try to grasp the secrets they keep.

So here I float in this quirky stream,
Chasing giggles, just living the dream.
Through currents of joy, I glide with glee,
In this wild tapestry made just for me.

Breath of Ferns and Secrets

Among the ferns, I take a breath,
In shadows where whispers tease at death.
A hedgehog does an acrobatic spin,
Saying, "Life's a circus, come on in!"

With secrets tucked beneath the moss,
I ponder my choices, a minor toss.
A squirrel's advice is a toss-up too,
When nutty ideas shoot out like glue.

A breeze giggles, it's hard to ignore,
As I step on quiet paths to explore.
Birds trade gossip, quite the scandal fest,
While I'm left wondering, who's the best?

So here I sit, in my leafy throne,
Amidst laughable antics, I feel right at home.
With a wink from the daisies as I recline,
Life here is odd, yet completely divine.

Awakening the Primal Within

In the depths, a beast does stir,
With a snort and a goofy purr.
It wiggles and jiggles with glee,
Hooting at branches, so wild and free.

Paws tapping lightly, a dance quite rare,
Swinging from branches without a care.
Silly antics that draw the eyes,
Waiting for snacks in cloudy skies.

With a rumble and tumble, all in fun,
Chasing shadows, we laugh and run.
A roar turns into a ticklish tease,
In the chaos, we find our ease.

Life's just a joke in this leafy land,
With a wink and a grin, we take a stand.
Poking at thorns, with giggles abound,
In the wild, our giggles resound!

Cries of the Hidden Sanctuary

A squirrel in a suit, what a sight,
Practices speeches all day and night.
Cracking jokes with grasshoppers near,
They chuckle and chirp, oh what a cheer!

Hidden away, where laughter blooms,
Choruses sing in playful rooms.
The hedgehogs giggle under the moon,
While bouncing to the rhythm, oh what a tune!

A peacock struts, with flair it thrives,
Telling tall tales of their crazy lives.
All the critters gather 'round with glee,
Telling wild secrets among the trees.

With a flick and a flap, they dance and play,
Every branch a stage, bright as day.
The echoes of joy, they softly stay,
In the heart where lullabies sway.

The Wild Echoes of Identity

A tiger with stripes that twist and turn,
Flips and flops, like it's time to learn.
It roars a laugh, with a belly so round,
In the echoes of fun, our giggles abound.

In this quirky place, a parrot sings,
About silly hats and other strange things.
Feathers and beaks, oh what a scene,
Making mischief like kings and queens!

A dance-off breaks near the old oak tree,
With vines as the judges, quite a spree!
The boogie woogie spreads wide and far,
Even the fireflies join in the bazaar.

Each echo reflects a whimsical truth,
Our true selves dancing, reclaiming our youth.
In this circus of whim, we find our might,
Laughter unraveling, pure delight!

Mosaics of the Inner Terrain

The lizards gossip with stylish flair,
Wearing tiny glasses in their wild lair.
With colors bright, they prance about,
On this canvas of fun, there's no doubt.

Frogs croak rhymes, with tongues a-twirl,
Ribbiting rhythms that make us whirl.
A cacophony bursting with silly cheer,
Our inner landscapes feel so near.

In this vivid maze of laughter's delight,
Squirrels build castles made of pure light.
Each twig a treasure in our wild space,
We dance on the paths at our own pace.

Every corner holds a zany surprise,
With pirates of fun in goofy disguise.
Together we mold this playful terrain,
In our hearts, the wild will remain!

The Call of Untamed Longing

In my heart, a wild beast roams,
Dancing 'round in papered tomes.
It craves a feast of joy and fun,
But finds a couch, and there it's done.

It howls at night for snacks and treats,
While I ignore its rambunctious beats.
Oh, to chase those paper snacks,
Instead, I nap, and dream of tracks.

Lost in dreams of grassy plains,
Where laughter flows like summer rains.
Yet here I sit, with chips in hand,
As the feral urges just expand.

This yearning beast curls up and snores,
While I remain, behind closed doors.
One day I'll let it roam and play,
But first, I need another day.

Portraits of a Hidden Soul

In mirrors, faces strangely blend,
One's a warrior, one's a friend.
They squabble fierce, then share a snack,
Together they plot a cheeky act.

A canvas filled with tangled dreams,
Where logic bends and laughter screams.
Brush strokes dance across the mind,
Painting madness, laughter entwined.

Each portrait tells a tale absurd,
Like fighting squirrels who misheard.
They steal my thoughts, they steal my snacks,
And in my dreams, they have no tracks.

So here I stand, a masterpiece,
With wild giggles that never cease.
Within this jumbled soul's display,
Lies a heart that loves to play.

Echoes of the Lost Expedition

We set out brave, in shorts and hats,
With snacks galore to share with cats.
An adventure through the living room,
Unleashing giggles, laughter, and zoom!

We journeyed far, past pillows high,
And feasted on some chocolate pie.
But maps got lost in messy piles,
And filled the world with goofy smiles.

Expeditions turn to silly quests,
As we discover couch fort nests.
Our compass spins, our laughter thrums,
While dogs take charge with playful hums.

At last we find our way back home,
With tales to share, like kings we roam.
Though maps may fade and snacks run low,
Our hearts will dance wherever we go.

Beneath the Canopy of Thought

Beneath the leaves of daily grind,
A circus stirs within my mind.
Monkeys swing from scattered lines,
While thoughts take flight like silly mimes.

A web of dreams, all tangled tight,
Where laughter sparks like fireflies bright.
Ideas bloom like flowers rare,
Yet sometimes, they just float in air.

A parade of whacky thoughts emerge,
With unicycle cats that laugh and surge.
Through tangled branches, I explore,
As giggles dance from core to core.

So let me wander, let me play,
In this wild world, I find my way.
For underneath this playful cover,
Lies a truth that comes from laughter.

Roots of the Inner Beasts

Deep in my mind, they wiggle and squirm,
Little fur critters that love to confirm.
With giggles and growls, they frolic about,
Snacking on thoughts that I can't live without.

A raccoon in shoes, quite stylish indeed,
Dances in dreams, planting mischief like seeds.
Their laughter resounds like a chorus so grand,
Life's simpler joys, at my command.

The wisdom of otters, they float on my streams,
Pop bubbles of worries, just follow your dreams.
In every odd corner, there's magic to find,
Just listen to whispers—the humor's so kind.

In this playground of whims, where chaos does dwell,
Each heartbeat a rhythm, a jolly good spell.
So, wiggle those roots, let your spirits erupt,
For joy lives wild, and we'll never give up.

Symphony of the Underbrush

Sashay through the leaves, a parade here unfolds,
With crickets on trumpets, and laughter that rolls.
The chatter of chipmunks, a witty concert,
Each note is a nibble, a cheerful dessert.

Bees doing ballet in a swirl of spring light,
Bumble and tumble, what a whimsical sight!
A chorus of frogs takes the stage with a splash,
To rhythmically croak, with a jubilant thrash.

Butterflies flutter in shades of bright hue,
They gossip and giggle, 'What are we to do?'
Twirling in circles, a playful ballet,
Nature's weird antics are just on display.

So come join the fun in this leafy cabaret,
Where secrets are shared in the sun's golden ray.
With each swish and sway, let your worries depart,
For laughter's the music that dances in heart.

Lurking in the Green

In emerald shades, something stirs in the gloom,
Peeking through bushes, plotting from their room.
A mischievous monkey, swinging on a vine,
Hoots out a riddle that's simply divine.

Chameleons giggle, they change just for kicks,
From green to bright pink, they play all their tricks.
While sloths roll their eyes, in a slow-motion daze,
Taking their time, while forming their crazy maze.

Alligators lounging, they sport funky shades,
Sipping on good times, in their swampy parades.
With glares and sly grins, they bask in the sun,
To them, life's a playground just waiting for fun.

So venture with glee into foliage's grasp,
The critters are waiting with jokes that they clasp.
In shadows or sunlight, let merriment reign,
For laughter's the treasure that dances in grain.

Colors of the Wild Heart

A dash of pink here, a splash of blue there,
Nature's a painter with whimsical flair.
Tigers in pajamas, they roam with finesse,
Posing for selfies in their bright, furry dress.

Parrots yacht along in feathers so bright,
Chattering nonsense from morning till night.
Bouncing in rhythm like popcorn on heat,
With jokes so hilarious, they're hard to beat.

Giraffes play limbo, necks bending with grace,
While zebras in stripes begin a merry race.
Every corner's alive with a silly parade,
Where humor and joy are splendidly made.

So let your heart wander where colors collide,
In rainbows of laughter, let sprites be your guide.
For each twist and turn brings a chuckle anew,
In this garden of giggles, let's frolic on through.

Hidden Alchemy of Flora

In a patch of green, where I trip and slide,
Petunias giggle, and daisies hide.
A sunflower winks, I can't help but stare,
"Join the dance, it's a flowery affair!"

Cacti wear hats made of bits of old string,
While roses gossip about the latest bling.
A fern does the cha-cha, it's quite a sight,
The daisies shout, "Stay all night!"

Vines twist and tangle, they play for keeps,
Mushrooms laugh softly, a secret they keep.
Nature's a carnival, wild and free,
Where every leaf's a whimsical decree!

Dandelions puff, they blow out a wish,
They snicker and share a giggly swish.
In this garden of jest, oh what a show,
The flora's alchemy is fun, you know!

Voices from the Thorns

In the thickets deep, there's laughter so spry,
Thorns whisper secrets beneath the sky.
"Watch your step, or you might become
The punchline here, just look at the fun!"

Bramble bush says with a prickly grin,
"Come join us, mate, let the mischief begin!"
Thorns can be sharp, but they also can tease,
"Just beware of your pants, if you please!"

A hedgehog chuckles with spines in a mess,
"Heard your last joke... it needs some finesse!"
But laughter still blooms from the prickly embrace,
Each thorny retort a dear friend's face.

With all this jesting, there's no room for fright,
In the thorns, my dear, it's a comedy night.
When life gets too serious, just heed the call,
The thorns have the funniest tales of all!

Mysterious Canopies

Above in the canopy, branches entwine,
Squirrels debate how to dine like fine wine.
"Should we go with acorns or peanuts today?"
They plot in the shadows, come join their buffet!

Who knew that the leaves had such clever discourse?
With puns and with stories, they gather, of course.
A parrot squawks tales of worm's wild escape,
While laughter cascades like a playful drape.

The mossy green floor serves as cushy seats,
Where beetles tell jokes that are sure to repeat.
"Why did the twig break up with the leaf?
Too much branch drama, oh what a belief!"

In this overhead world, shadows do sway,
With secrets and giggles that brighten the day.
When hours drift by in this leafy embrace,
The canopies chuckle, each grinning face.

Beneath the Rustling Leaves

Beneath rustling leaves, the fun never stops,
Crickets compose their own jazz-flavored pops.
"Join our band if you've got the right moves,"
A leaf drops and giggles, it totally groves!

Acorns roll by, sharing all of their loot,
"Have you tried juggling with a nut for a hoot?"
The squirrels just nod, they know how to play,
As laughter erupts in a nutty ballet.

The wind hums a tune, a whimsical sound,
While fungi create a soft, squishy ground.
"Tell me a joke, or just share a laugh,
As we troll through this woodland, let's craft our own path!"

With branches above as the stage for the show,
Nature's comedians steal each little glow.
Under these leaves, oh what fun it brings,
The rustles of joy are the best kind of swings!

Spirit of the Overgrowth

In a forest, thick and curly,
Trees wear coats of emerald furry.
Squirrels plot with acorns tight,
Whispers echo, day turns night.

Frogs in tuxes leap with grace,
To impress that croaking face.
Laughter bounces in the air,
Even vines have jokes to share.

Mushrooms hiding, nodding heads,
Rooted dreams in cozy beds.
Worms do waltzes underground,
Joyful pulses all around.

Creature parties, what a sight!
In the shadow, feeling light.
Nature's laughter, sweet and loud,
A wild, wacky, leafy crowd.

Breath of the Lush

Whimsical winds suggest a dance,
As ferns sway, oh what a chance!
Bamboo giggles in the breeze,
Tickling grasses, ever pleased.

Parrots chat with raucous cheer,
While chameleons shift, oh dear!
Mossy carpets, plush and bright,
Slip and slide, a funny fright!

Beetles band, an off-key song,
Fluffy bunnies hop along.
Giggling leaves, they twist and turn,
In this play, all creatures learn.

Raccoons wear the finest hats,
Crafted from the fallen mats.
Joy abounds in every nook,
Life's a merry, green storybook.

Dances of the Hidden

Underbrush holds secrets tight,
Mice in tails, a playful sight.
Pandas pirouette just so,
While fireflies dance with the glow.

Sloths slide down to join the fun,
Trusty tails come out to run.
Twigs snap under tiny feet,
With chuckles sweet, they can't be beat.

Bears in berets lead the show,
As the tiny insects flow.
A waltz of wonder, gleeful mobs,
Nature's talent, here and sobs.

Critters clapping all around,
To rhythm lost but newly found.
The lilting forest plays its tune,
A happy jig beneath the moon.

Navigating the Wildwood

Get your maps, the paths are wild,
Navigators, giggle and smiled.
With branches swaying overhead,
Do squirrels lead? Or charm instead?

Raccoons plot with cheesy flair,
While owls hoot without a care.
Tangled foliage greets the roam,
Adventure calls, and it feels like home!

The roots twist up, a funny maze,
Try and find your way through haze.
Laughter echoes through the glade,
Nature's fun, our grand parade.

So take a left where daisies bloom,
Or find a clearing with room.
Amidst the whimsy, let's explore,
The wildwood beckons, who could ask for more?

Cradled by Nature's Rhythm

In the heart of the trees, where the critters play,
A squirrel does ballet, in a charming ballet.
Frogs croak the tunes, with their throaty croons,
While raccoons tap dance under the glowing moons.

Branches sway gently, a tree's joyful flare,
A parrot plays tricks with a mischievous stare.
Laughter fills air, with the sound of a breeze,
Nature's own symphony, if you please!

Giraffes make a line, like a long conga train,
While elephants stomp, causing a playful rain.
Chasing the shadows, they twirl and spin,
In this raucous revel, let the fun begin!

As the sun sets low, painting skies aglow,
The creatures all gather, for a wild show.
With grins on their faces, they join the feast,\nIn the rhythm of nature, we all find the least.

Serenade of the Untamed Spirit

A wild cat sings softly, a jazzy refrain,
While monkeys throw parties, causing sweet mayhem.
With bananas for maracas, they shake to the beat,
And the sloths slowly sway, thinking it's neat.

Bees buzz in harmony, humming along,
With a chorus of frogs, croaking a song.
The turtles join in, though they're never in rush,
Adding to beats with their gentle hush.

A lizard in shades, strikes a cool pose,
And the ants do the cha-cha right up to their toes.
Each creature a player in this wacky parade,
Here in the wild, let shenanigans cascade!

As night blankets all, a chill in the air,
Creatures gather 'round, without a single care.
Under twinkling stars, they dance with delight,
In the serenade of spirits, everything's right.

Unraveling the Mystery of Shades

In the dappled light where the shadows play,
A raccoon's clever plan goes hilariously astray.
He thinks he's a ninja, sneaky and sly,
But trips on a twig, oh me, oh my!

An owl provides wisdom, but mostly just snacks,
While beetles roll peanuts along quaint tracks.
The mystery deepens as the sun starts to fade,
Who'll win the talent show? All bets are made.

The chameleons change, but their dance is the same,
Like colorful ninjas, without any shame.
They groove to the rhythm of the forest's delight,
While fireflies wink, making the night bright.

And as we unwrap this curious place,
Laughter erupts, a jubilant embrace.
In every dark corner, and in every hue,
The silly reveals itself, hidden from view.

Dreams Woven in the Canopy

Nestled high up, in a leafy retreat,
A dreaming koala has rustled his seat.
With visions of eucalyptus twirling around,
He sleeps through the antics of beasts all around.

A dreaming old sloth, in a hammock he swings,
Imagines he's king, ruling over all things.
While the monkeys devise a banana heist,
His dreams are of lunch, oh isn't that nice?

An opossum plays dead, it's just his old trick,
While the parrots squawk gossip, oh give me a break!
All around the branches, delight fills the air,
In this leafy dreamland, none have a care.

As the sun peeks through, painting colors so bright,
Creatures awaken to their glorious plight.
They laugh at the dreams, as silly might seem,
In the canopy's cradle, we all live the dream!

Paths through the Undergrowth

In the quiet nook where the wild things roam,
A squirrel wears glasses, stealing my comb.
A hedgehog in slippers is dancing the night,
While ants in tuxedos hold quite the sight.

The flowers are gossiping, swaying with glee,
As frogs in top hats throw a grand jamboree.
The wind whispers secrets, tickling my nose,
While vines gossip loudly, like overgrown pros.

A caterpillar dreams of a life on a train,
While bugs play charades in the midst of the rain.
In this whimsical world, let's not act so shy,
Join the creatures, dear friend—let's give it a try!

For paths through the undergrowth twist and they turn,
With laughter and antics, there's much to discern.
So skip through the foliage, let worries be few,
In this wild, funny place, there's always room for two.

Reflections in the Rainforest

In puddles of laughter, we find our own tales,
Where parrots in bowties flaunt colorful scales.
The monkeys bring snacks, and they start a green feast,
While sloths play the drums, keeping time at the least.

A toucan with style declares, "I'm the best!"
As iguanas tango, oh, aren't they impressed?
With leaves for a dance floor and vines as a stage,
The creatures all gather, unleashing their rage.

The rain's soft percussion, a beat so delightful,
Critters take turns with moves so insightful.
And through funny reflections, we see our own grin,
Awakening joy from the chaos within.

So splash in the puddles, let giggles take flight,
In this realm of reflections, oh, what a sight!
With nothing but wonder, the forest sings loud,
Join the merry party, together, be proud!

Veins of Nature's Pulse

In the heart of the green, where laughter is spun,
A rabbit in sneakers says, 'Ready, set, run!'
With vines as our guides and the sun as our lamp,
We dash through the foliage, like kids at a camp.

A chameleon wiggles, "I'm blending in still!"
While a turtle in shades poses over the hill.
The rhythm of life is a dance, oh so sweet,
With flowers and fungi just bringing the beat.

Frogs croaking selfies, they're hip as can be,
As leaves do the cha-cha, quite joyfully free.
The buzzing of bees creates just the right tune,
In this pulse of the wild, we sway with the moon.

With laughter aplenty, we'll rush and we'll twirl,
For veins of nature connect every girl,
And boy, in the chaos where funny prevails,
We'll dance through the green, on wild, wacky trails.

Tangles of Forgotten Dreams

In the depths of the thicket, where whimsy can sway,
A raccoon in pajamas starts a cabaret.
With shadows as partners, the owls cheer and clap,
While fireflies flicker like stars on a map.

A toad on a lily holds court with a grin,
As stories of mischief swirl up from within.
The vines wrap around, like old friends in a hug,
While crickets compose a song, snug as a bug.

From the depths of the past, where the wild dreams take shape,
A parrot tells echoes of bananas and tape.
These tangles remind us of laughter long lost,
In the banter of blossoms, we learn what it costs.

So come weave with the wild, let the giggles unfold,
In the realm of forgotten, where magic is bold.
For the dreams are still dancing, like leaves in the breeze,
In this tangled-up world, there's joy that can please.

Visions of the Untrodden Path

A squirrel in a hat, quite the sight,
Dances around, oh what a delight!
Chasing his shadow, leaps with glee,
While birds laugh loudly, sipping their tea.

Beneath the big tree, a cat plays chess,
With a wise old owl, they both dress to impress.
Each move is a joke, each pause a jest,
In this odd game, they both are the best.

An ant with a trumpet, a fancy parade,
Leading his friends in a quirky charade.
Marching in rhythm, they twist and they sway,
Creating a ruckus to brighten the day.

In this world of wonder, laughter ignites,
As beasts in bow ties share silly insights.
With chuckles and giggles, life's just a play,
On this wild, untrodden, hilarious way.

Roar of Introspection

A lion with glasses sips on green tea,
Wondering if he's too roary, you see.
He ponders his mane, does it shine or fade?
With each thoughtful sip, it begins to cascade.

A parrot teaches yoga, poses with flair,
In a tree with a mirror, they both stop and stare.
"Just breathe!" he squawks while standing on one,
Balancing life under the jungle sun.

Deep in the bushes, a rabbit writes prose,
Jotting down dreams only he truly knows.
Between nibbling carrots, he jots with a wink,
"What if I flew?" Oh, how his thoughts sink!

Amidst all the chatter, reflection rides high,
Creatures chuckle deeply, as clouds drift by.
For laughter can heal, it fills up the soul,
Even lions, wise owls, and rabbits want polls.

Cries of the Inner Wilderness

An elephant sneezes, the ground shakes and quakes,
Followed by five monkeys who dive in lakes.
They bubble and splash, what a curious scene,
As one does a backflip, and lands on a bean.

A hippo does ballet, with a tutu of leaves,
Spinning 'round gracefully, while the jungle grieves.
"Oh dear!" says a turtle, "Is that a hip-hop?"
As he checks his own moves, and ends with a plop.

In the brush, a ferret invents a new game,
Where each playful tumble earns you wild fame.
With giggles and rolls, they tumble around,
In this wilderness where joy knows no bound.

They sing out in chorus, "Where's the next snack?"
While owls hoot softly, who'll say, "Not back!"
For in these cries, a hilarity grows,
A riot of laughter that only one knows.

Landscapes of the Soul's Brush

Colors of chaos paint the trees bright,
As llamas wear goggles, taking flight.
They hover through colors, a sight to behold,
While frogs paint with voices, so fearless and bold.

A hipster chameleon switched to plaid,
Declares, "I'm just vibing, nothing is bad!"
While sipping on smoothies of tropical fruits,
His friends all agree, in their quirky suits.

While rainbows splice the sky like a dream,
And goldfish juggle, plotting their scheme.
They cast funny wishes in ripples that sway,
Wishing for smiles in their own special way.

With whimsy and wonder, their laughter flows,
In this painted paradise, anything goes.
In the landscapes of joy, such humor takes root,
In a colorful world, life's playful pursuit.

The Forest of Forgotten Whispers

In the woods where secrets play,
Squirrels gossip night and day.
Lost socks dance on branches high,
While rabbits laugh as nutty pies fly.

Beneath a tree, a frog wears shoes,
Singing songs of silly blues.
The owls wink in puzzling layers,
Crickets form a band of players.

Mushrooms giggle in a row,
Ticklish vines start to grow.
Come find the laughter in the bark,
Where whispers sing at dawn's first spark.

Join the chat in leafy halls,
With chirps and caws, the laughter calls.
For in this wood, we all belong,
A chorus bright, where all is wrong!

Splendor of the Inner Grove

Among the trees, a party thrived,
Frogs in hats, oh how they jived!
Leaves of gold twirl in the breeze,
While chipmunks bust some dance moves with ease.

A funky bear with mismatched socks,
Breaks it down, surprising the ox.
The rhythm beats through roots and twigs,
As owls hoot out their silly digs.

Fireflies wink, like disco lights,
As hedgehogs plan their silly flights.
A rabbit DJ spins with flair,
In this grove, we've not a care!

Mirthful sounds of laughter blend,
While nature's music has no end.
Come join the fun, don't stay aloof,
You'll find your groove beneath this roof!

Thickets of Unsung Melody

In thickets dense, the critters meet,
Where shadows dance to a tin can beat.
Raccoons trade their shiny loot,
While ferns sway to a rhythmic hoot.

The unstrung lute lies by the creek,
A caterpillar's dreams unique.
Bumblebees hum a bouncy tune,
As fireflies flicker 'neath the moon.

A hedgehog croons with a quirky flair,
While bushes sway without a care.
In this thicket, joy takes flight,
With every laugh, the world feels bright.

Gather 'round, the music flows,
With every note, the laughter grows.
In thickets where the wild things play,
Let's dance and sing our cares away!

Lullabies from the Wild Unknown

Where shadows creep and giggles roam,
A nighttime song, that feels like home.
The breeze whispers tales of the day,
As critters join in a soft ballet.

Under stars that twinkle bright,
A raccoon strums the moonlit night.
While sleepy spiders spin their dreams,
And fireflies waltz in glittering streams.

A sleepy fox with crazy hair,
Breaks into dance without a care.
The lullabies of night befall,
As twinkling whispers serenade all.

So drift away in this wild hush,
As laughter fades in a gentle thrush.
Snooze in peace 'till morning light,
In the wild unknown, all feels right!

www.ingramcontent.com/pod-product-compliance
Lightning Source LLC
Chambersburg PA
CBHW070310120526
44590CB00017B/2613